Exploring Science

The Exploring Science series is designed to meet all the Attainment Targets in the National Science Curriculum for levels 3 to 6. The topics in each book are divided into knowledge and understanding sections, followed by exploration. Carefully planned Test Yourself questions at the end of each topic ensure that the student has mastered the appropriate level of attainment specified in the Curriculum.

EXPLORING
USES OF ENERGY

Ed Catherall

Wayland

Exploring Science

Exploring Earth in Space
Exploring Electricity
Exploring Energy Sources
Exploring Forces and Structures
Exploring Habitats
Exploring Humans and the Environment
Exploring Information Technology
Exploring Light
Exploring Magnets
Exploring Ourselves
Exploring Plants
Exploring Soil and Rocks
Exploring Sound
Exploring Uses of Energy
Exploring Variety of Life
Exploring Weather

Cover illustrations:
Above left *A diagram to show how forces balance on a seesaw.*
Above right *Water being boiled over a gas burner.*
Below *As he cycles, the cyclist transfers his stored energy into kinetic energy.*

Frontispiece *A judo player uses his body as a lever to throw his opponent off balance.*

Editor: Elizabeth Spiers
Series designer: Ross George

First published in 1990 by
Wayland (Publishers) Ltd
61 Western Road, Hove
East Sussex BN3 1JD, England

British Library Cataloguing in Publication Data
Catherall, Ed *1931–*
   Exploring uses of energy.
   1. Uses of energy
   I. Title II. Series
   531.6

HARDBACK ISBN 1–85210–839–8

PAPERBACK ISBN 0–7502–0574–1

Typeset by R. Gibbs & N. Taylor, Wayland
Printed in Italy by G. Canale & C.S.p.A., Turin

Contents

ENERGY FOR LIFE

At every moment in your life, you are using energy. Whether you are asleep or actively awake, you are using the chemical energy from food. This is an energy store, just like a fuel such as petrol or coal.

Your body is like a car engine. The car uses oxygen from the air to burn petrol, releasing the energy stored in the petrol so that the car can move. You 'burn' food inside your body's cells, and you also need oxygen to do this. The energy is released from the food, so that your body can work. The more work you do, the more energy your body needs. Food also provides the raw materials to build and repair your body, and to keep it in good health.

All our food comes from green plants. They are able to convert the Sun's energy into food. We can eat green plants directly, or we can eat animals that have themselves eaten green plants and are, therefore, an energy store.

This energy transfer is called a food chain. Without the Sun and green plants, we would be unable to live, as we need energy for life.

These children are enjoying a wide variety of food at a birthday party. However, food is eaten not only for enjoyment but to build up energy stores.

ACTIVITIES

PULSE RATE

YOU NEED

• **a watch with a second hand**

---

1 Find your pulse in your wrist or neck. Count how many beats you can feel in one minute, while you stand very still.

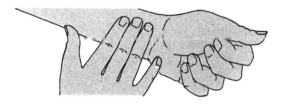

2 Do this several times. Is your rate the same?
3 Repeat this timing while reading a book.
4 Repeat it when you are lying down.
5 Run around the playground. Take your pulse as soon as you stop. Take it again, 5 minutes later.

When pulse taken	counts per minute
Immediately after running	
5 minutes after running	

6 How is your pulse rate affected by each different activity?

BREATHING RATE

1 Try to breathe normally and evenly. Count the number of breaths that you take in 1 minute. Do this several times. Is the rate the same each time?
2 Repeat this while reading a book, then lying down.
3 Do the running activity in the same way as you did when checking your pulse rate. This time, count your breathing rates. What do you notice?
4 Is there any relationship between your pulse rate and breathing rate?

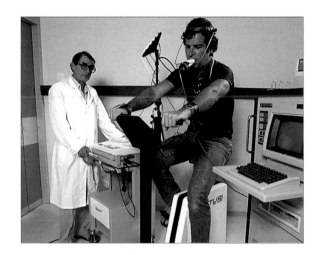

This ultrasound heart-rate machine shows how the heart works during exercise.

TEST YOURSELF

1. How is your body like a car engine?
2. What does your body use as fuel?
3. Explain how the Sun provides your body with energy.

WORKING HARD

Are you active today? If so, you are using a lot of energy. You need energy to move. Whenever you push, pull, roll or move your body in any way, you are working. You need energy to be able to work. The more work you do, the more energy you use.

The world is full of energy in different forms. Heat energy and light energy, which travel to us from the Sun, are two forms of energy. Another form is electrical energy, which travels to us from power stations. Yet another form is sound energy, which travels to our ears and causes us to hear.

Mechanical energy is the energy of movement. When a ball is thrown in the air it is given energy. This type of energy, which involves something actually moving, is called kinetic energy. Mechanical energy can also be

These people are working out in a gymnasium. They are using kinetic energy to move the bicycles and weights.

stored. If you climb to the top of a slide and sit there you have stored the energy you used to get there. You might decide to move at any time, so you need this energy store. If you then let go, the stored energy is changed back into kinetic energy as you move from the top of the slide to the bottom. This type of stored energy is called potential energy.

Your energy comes from food, which contains another type of stored energy called chemical energy. It is called chemical energy because it is stored within the chemical structure of a substance. Food is a fuel. All fuels contain stored energy.

ACTIVITY

WORKING IN THE PLAYGROUND

This girl gains potential energy as she swings up.

> ### YOU NEED
>
> • **a playground with a slide, swing and seesaw**

1 Climb up the steps of the slide. As you climb you are using kinetic energy.
2 Stop at the top of the steps. You are now full of potential energy.
3 Get on to the slide and slide down. What has happened to your potential energy?

4 Sit on a swing. Work it so that you go higher and higher. Think about the types of energy you have as you swing.
5 Which type of energy do you have at the top of the swing, when it is still for a moment?
6 What type of energy do you have before you start your swinging?
7 Get on to the seesaw with a friend. Work the seesaw together. Which types of energy are you and your friend using?

This girl is turning potential energy into kinetic energy.

> WARNING: playgrounds can be dangerous if you do not use the equipment properly.

TEST YOURSELF

1. What is kinetic energy?
2. What is potential energy?
3. Give an example of potential energy being changed into kinetic energy.

BALANCING A SEESAW

A seesaw is a long plank balanced in the middle. This balance point is called the fulcrum. A seesaw with no-one sitting on it should be perfectly balanced. If you sit on one end of the seesaw, it will go down, because you exert a force (your weight). If a friend sits on the other side of the seesaw it can be made to balance again. When this happens, you have both done work.

Work is done when a force moves. Your weight is the force on one side of the seesaw. The work done by you is your weight multiplied by your distance from the fulcrum. Your friend also has weight and so is exerting a force on the seesaw.

The seesaw can be balanced if your friend weighs the same as you, and if he or she sits at the same distance from the fulcrum on one side as you are on the other side. However, the chances are that your friend is not the same weight as you, but is either lighter or heavier. In spite of this, you can both get the seesaw to balance if one of you moves along it. The seesaw will balance when:

weight of your friend x distance from fulcrum = your weight x distance from fulcrum

When the seesaw balances, the work done on one side equals the work done on the other side.

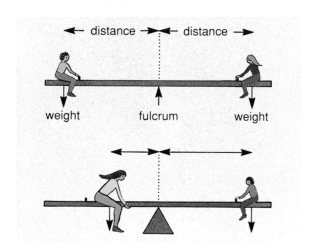

Above *The diagram shows how a seesaw can be balanced when both people weigh the same (top), and when one person is heavier than the other.*

Left *A tug-of-war is won by the team that can make the larger force. If both teams create the same force, the rope stays 'balanced', and neither team wins.*

ACTIVITY

YOU NEED

- **a ruler**
- **a pencil**
- **several identical coins**

1 Place the pencil on the table. Balance the ruler on the pencil, so that the ruler acts as a seesaw.
2 Find the fulcrum on your ruler. Remember to take all your measurements from the fulcrum.

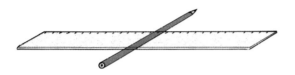

3 Put one coin 2 cm from the fulcrum. Check that the 2 cm mark passes through the middle of the coin.

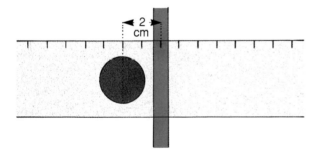

4 Put another coin on the other side of the fulcrum. Move it until the seesaw balances. How far is the middle of the coin from the fulcrum?
5 Move one coin to the 4 cm mark. Where do you have to place the other coin to balance your seesaw?
6 Move the coin to other positions. Balance the ruler each time.
7 Place two coins on top of each other, 2 cm from the fulcrum. Where do you have to put one coin on the other side in order to balance these 2 coins? Try other positions.

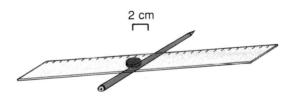

8 What is the largest number of coins that you can balance with one coin?
9 Check all your results, using the information on page 10. Count the weight of each coin as 1. Do your experiments follow the rule?

TEST YOURSELF

1. What is the fulcrum?
2. When does a seesaw balance?
3. If you put 3 coins at the 2 cm mark on a seesaw, where do you have to place one coin on the other side, so that the seesaw balances? Check your answer by doing it.

ENERGY IS USED TO LIFT A LOAD

If you grasp a friend around the waist you may be able to lift her off the ground, but it takes a lot of effort, or force. It is almost impossible to lift two friends at the same time. Together, your friends may weigh twice as much as you do and you cannot provide enough muscular force to lift them. However, if both friends sit on one side of a seesaw and you sit on the other side, you can lift them easily. They just have to sit nearer to the fulcrum than you are. To lift your two friends, you must make the work done on your side of the seesaw greater than the work done on your friends' side. Work done = force x distance (see page 10) and you have greatly increased your distance from the fulcrum.

In this activity you are using the seesaw as a lever to raise your friends into the air. A lever is a simple machine that, used in this way, reduces the amount of force, or effort, needed. A lever does not reduce the amount of work done. The work is the same; the lever just saves effort. A lever may be used to lift heavy weights, such as when a crowbar is used to move rocks. A screwdriver can be used as a lever to prise open a tightly-fitting paint-can lid. A crane on a building site also works as a lever.

Notice that there are counterweights on one side of a lever. You are the counterweight on the seesaw.

Sometimes, levers are used in pairs. Pliers, scissors, shears and wire-cutters are all pairs of levers. They have long handles on one side of the fulcrum to provide the extra force on the other side.

A pole-vaulter uses the pole as a lever to lift his weight over the bar.

ACTIVITY

USING LEVERS

YOU NEED

- **a block of wood**
- **a claw hammer**
- **nails**

1 Hold the hammer at the end of the handle. Hammer a nail into the wood.

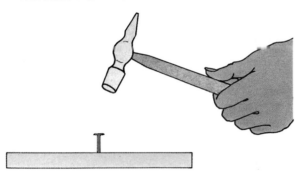

2 Hammer another nail into the wood. This time, hold the handle of the hammer in the middle.

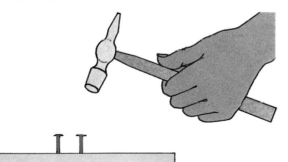

3 Which nail was easier to hammer in? Why?

4 What happens if you hold the hammer very close to the metal head, so that you have a short handle?

5 Use the claw end of the hammer to pull the nails out. Notice how the claw acts as a lever. Where is the best place to hold the hammer to pull out the nails?

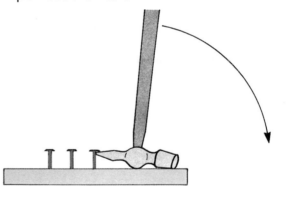

WARNING: be very careful when using tools of any sort.

TEST YOURSELF

1. Explain how one person can lift two people on a seesaw.
2. What is a lever?
3. Describe how you would use a lever to lift a heavy rock.

TYPES OF LEVER

Levers can be divided into three types, or classes. The most common is the first-class lever, which works like a seesaw. The load (or force) is on one side, while the effort (the other force) is on the other side. The effort is made in one direction, while the load moves in the other direction. In order to lift up the load, you have to press down on the other side of the lever. A pair of pliers is a first-class lever. This kind of lever reduces the force needed to do a job.

A second-class lever has the effort and load on the same side of the fulcrum. The fulcrum is at one end of the lever. To use a second-class lever, you have to make the effort in the same direction in which you want the load to move. To find out the work done, you still measure the distance from the effort to the fulcrum and from the load to the fulcrum. This lever is most efficient when the load is close to the fulcrum. Wheelbarrows and doors are second-class levers.

A third-class lever also has the fulcrum at one end, with the load and effort on the same side. Here, the load is at the end of the lever while the effort is near the fulcrum (the opposite of a second-class lever). If you measure the work done, you will see that this is not an efficient machine. This is because a large effort is needed to move a small load. However, provided that the load is small, a large effort can be used to move it over a long distance. When you swing a golf club at a golf ball, you are using a third-class lever. The ball is the load, while your hands, arms and body provide the effort to hit the ball over a great distance.

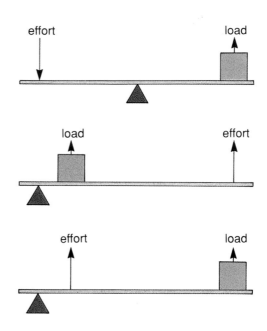

Above *The three types of lever.*

Below *The golfer uses his club as a third-class lever.*

ACTIVITIES

USING A SECOND-CLASS LEVER

YOU NEED

- **a bottle opener**
- **two unopened soft-drink bottles**

1 Use the bottle opener to prise the metal cap off a soft-drink bottle. Where is the fulcrum of the bottle opener?

2 Notice that your effort and the force holding the cap to the bottle is on the same side of the fulcrum.

3 What happens if you try to open the bottle, holding the bottle opener near to the metal cap?

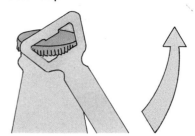

USING A THIRD-CLASS LEVER

YOU NEED

- **a pair of tweezers**
- **table-tennis bats**
- **a table-tennis ball and table**

1 Look at a pair of tweezers. Notice that the fulcrum is at one end. Notice where you are supposed to put your fingers.

2 Try picking up something using tweezers. Find out where it is hardest to hold the tweezers to pick up an object.

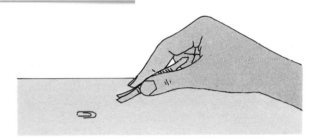

3 Play table tennis with a friend. Where is the fulcrum, your effort and the ball (the load) while you play?

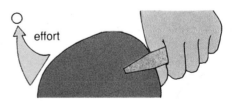

4 What do you do when you want to hit the ball hard, as in a smash?

TEST YOURSELF

1. Name another second-class lever and identify the load, effort and fulcrum.
2. Name another third-class lever. Describe how it is used.
3. Why is a second-class lever more efficient than a third-class lever?

WEDGES

An axe makes wood-chopping easier in two ways: the wedge increases the force and the handle acts as a lever.

Humans have been using levers for over 6,000 years to lift and throw objects. Once humans settled and learned how to farm, they used levers for many tasks. For example, the shadoof is a water-lifting machine. It is used to irrigate fields; the effort is on one side of the lever, while a bucket of water is the load on the other side. Another simple machine that was used thousands of years ago is the wedge. A wedge is a triangular-shaped block made of metal, stone or hard wood. The axe heads of Stone Age people were made of wedge-shaped pieces of flint.

A wedge is used for splitting. For example, if you want to split a log, you can put the narrow end of a metal wedge into a small slit in the log.

The wide end of the wedge is hit with a hammer. The force, or effort, applied at the wide end is increased as it goes through the wedge to the narrow cutting edge. So, in a way, the wedge is like a force-increasing lever.

You can also split the log by using an axe. An axe is a wedge on a handle. Here, you have the advantage of the wedge increasing the force, as well as the handle acting as a lever. This increases the force even more, so the Stone Age axe was a very efficient machine.

Today, we use a lot of wedge-shaped tools: for example, a knife and a chisel. Scissors are like a pair of chisels as well as a pair of first-class levers (see page 14). Nails, needles and pins are also types of wedge.

ACTIVITIES

YOU NEED

- **a wedge-shaped piece of hard wood**
- **a hammer**

1 Place your wedge just under the leg of a table.
2 Gently tap the thick end of the wedge with the hammer, so that the table just begins to rise up the wedge.
3 Ask a friend to sit on the table. Now gently tap the wedge again. Notice how the wedge not only lifts the table but your friend as well, with quite a gentle tap. Here a little effort is used to raise a big load.

WARNING: be very careful when using a hammer.

BITING AN APPLE

YOU NEED

- **an apple**
- **a mirror**

A set of healthy front teeth.

1 Look into a mirror while you bite into an apple. Your front teeth are wedge-shaped.
2 Notice how your teeth bite. What kind of paired levers are your front teeth? (Remember: they are part of your jaw.)

TEST YOURSELF

1. What is a wedge and how does it work?
2. Why is the bow of a ship wedge-shaped?
3. Explain why an axe is used to split logs.

DOING WORK IS USING ENERGY

Energy is the ability to do work. The more work you do, the more energy you need and use. You also tend to use more force to do more work.

We measure force in newtons and work done in joules. The amount of energy is also measured in joules, because you need energy to get work done. The definition of a newton is the force needed to give a mass of 1 kg an acceleration of 1 metre per second.

Kilograms are used to measure the mass, or the amount, of an object. If you stand on one side of a balance and kilogram masses are put on the other side until it is balanced, it is possible to measure the mass, or amount, of you in kilograms.

Weight is the pull of gravity on an object. This pull is the force of gravity and so it is measured in newtons. The force of gravity is different on other planets and moons, but on Earth, weight is about 10 x mass. For example, suppose your mass is 40 kilograms, your weight, due to the force of gravity, is 10 x 40 kg, or 400 newtons.

If you climb a vertical ladder 10 m high, you are 400 newtons climbing up against gravity for 10 m. The work done is 400 newtons (force) x 10 m (distance), which is 4,000 joules. You would need 4,000 joules of energy to do this climb.

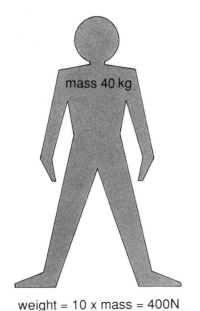

weight = 10 x mass = 400N

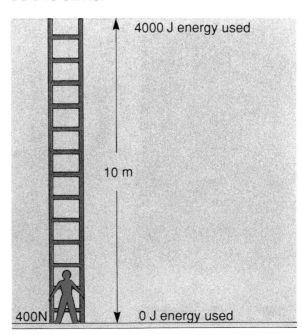

ACTIVITY

MEASURING FORCE

YOU NEED

- **a newtonmeter**
- **a book**
- **strong string**
- **a 1 kg mass with a hook**

1 Work with a friend. Look at your newtonmeter. It is used to measure force. Make sure that you both understand what the markings mean.

2 Tie a piece of string tightly to a door handle. Make a loop at the other end of the string for your newtonmeter hook.

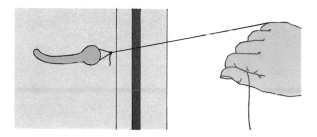

3 Hook the newtonmeter to the string. Make sure the door is slightly ajar. Pull the newtonmeter very gently, until the door begins to move. Your friend should watch the scale of the newtonmeter very carefully, and take the reading exactly when the door starts to move.

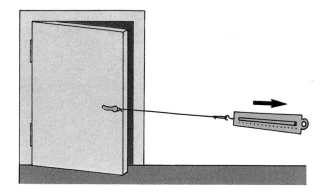

4 Hook the newtonmeter to the 1 kg mass. Lift the newtonmeter gently, and take a reading of the force.

5 Make a string cradle with a loop to fit round your book. Lift it gently with the newtonmeter. How much force did it take to do this?

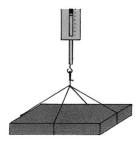

6 Repeat the experiment with a few more objects. Make a chart to show your results.

TEST YOURSELF

1. Which units do you use to measure energy?

2. If you are 500 newtons and you climb 10 metres vertically up a ladder, how much work have you done and how much energy have you used?

RAMPS

A wheelchair ramp in a hospital. It would take much greater effort to push this boy up a flight of steps.

Ramps are like wedges. When you use a wedge, it is the wedge that moves (see page 16). When you use a ramp, it stays still and the object moves, getting higher as it goes. Therefore, the object is being lifted, as well as being pushed along.

Ramps are used in many places. People in wheelchairs, pushing prams and moving objects on to lorries all need ramps. It is much harder to move up a step than to wheel an object up a ramp. More work must be done to climb steps, so more force is used, and more energy is needed.

Think of all the places where there are steps and stairs. All large buildings should have ramps for wheelchair and pram access. Look for them. Think of a journey that you make in town when you are walking. Could you make the same journey in a wheelchair? Are there ramps at every step?

A ramp is also called an inclined plane. When a slope is made of a plank of wood, you incline the wood to make a slope. The shallower the slope, the smaller the vertical distance that the load is raised. It is easier to push something up a long, shallow ramp than up a short, steep one.

Roads zigzag up steep hills. These roads are like ramps up the hill. Railways zigzag up mountains. Notice how a long staircase in a house will change direction (zigzag) to make shorter flights of stairs with flat rest areas (landings).

ACTIVITY

TESTING RAMPS

YOU NEED

- **a length of smooth wood**
- **a nail**
- **string**
- **books**
- **a heavy toy car or roller skate**
- **a ruler**
- **a plastic tub**
- **identical coins**

1 Make 3 holes near the top of the tub with the nail. Pass string through the holes to make a handle for the tub.

2 Tie a length of string to the front of the car and attach the other end to the handle of the tub.

3 Place your piece of wood on the edge of the table. Put the car on the wood and let the tub hang down over the edge of the table.
4 Put coins in the tub until the car starts to move. Record how many you used.

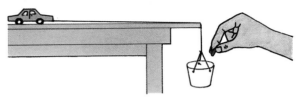

5 Place your wood on books to make a ramp.
6 Adjust the books until the top end of the ramp is 5 cm from the top of the table.
7 Put coins into the tub until the car starts to move up the ramp. Record this number.

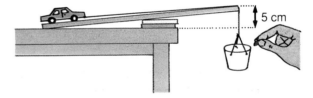

5 cm

8 Now adjust the ramp so that the top end is 10 cm high.
9 Repeat the experiment. Record the number of coins. Keep raising the ramp until it is nearly vertical. What do you notice about your results?

WARNING: be very careful when using the nail.

TEST YOURSELF

1. What is an inclined plane?
2. Why do roads zigzag up steep hills?
3. Why does water run faster down a steep slope than down a shallow slope?

CURVED RAMPS

You know that the shallower the slope of an inclined plane, the easier it is to lift a load (see page 20). However, there is often not enough room to make a long, straight, shallow slope. Rather than make a series of zigzagging roads up a steep hill, it is often easier to construct a spiral road that goes completely around the hill. To keep the slope shallow, the road can spiral round many times before it reaches the top of the hill. The vertical distance between each turn in the spiral is small.

Stairs in a house take up a lot of room that could be used as living space, especially if the house is tall. Spiral staircases take up less space. They are most often found in lighthouses and around lift shafts.

Spiral roads are put in multistorey car parks, to leave more space for parking. On a helter-skelter, you spiral down on a mat, giving you a longer, smoother ride. Many water theme parks have special slides inside spiral tubes.

Besides horizontal spirals, you can also have vertical spirals. On a roller-coaster ride the train often loops the loop. The train is towed to the top and then accelerates down due to gravity. It loops the loop on track that spirals vertically.

A spiral staircase is a curved ramp. Because the vertical distance between each turn in the spiral is quite small, the climb is less steep than it would be if the ramp led directly from the top to the bottom of the building.

ACTIVITY

YOU NEED

- **a metre length of clear plastic tubing**
- **a ruler**
- **a small marble that will roll inside the tubing**

1 Arrange your tube in a J-shape.
2 Release the marble from a vertical height of 10 cm on one side of the J-shape. How far up the other side of the arm does the marble go? What happens to the marble?
3 Release the marble at a vertical height of 15 cm. How far up the other arm of the J-shape does the marble go now?

4 Keep increasing the vertical height at which you release the marble.
5 Arrange the tubing in a J-shape so that one side is much higher than the other. What happens when you release the marble down the long side?

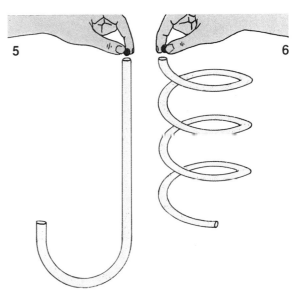

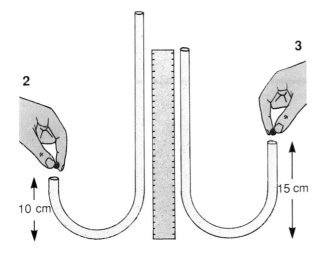

6 Arrange the tubing as a spiral, as if it were going around a hill. Release your marble at the top of the spiral. What happens to the speed of the marble as it travels down the spiral?
7 What do you have to do to make the vertical height of your spiral greater? Does the marble travel faster or slower than before in this new spiral?

TEST YOURSELF

1. Where can you find spiral staircases? What is the advantage of a spiral staircase?
2. Imagine that you are sitting on a mat at the top of a helter-skelter. Describe your ride down.
3. Describe how you could make a marble loop the loop. Try out your ideas.

SCREWS

A screw is a simple machine, because it saves effort. It is really a curved ramp. The thread around a screw is like the horizontal spiral of a helter-skelter. In a helter-skelter, the spiral stays still and you travel down it, while in a screw, it is the spiral that moves. It works like a wedge (see page 16) and can be used to penetrate (cut into) materials. The amount that the screw will penetrate in one turn depends on the vertical distance between the threads. Remember that if you decrease the distance that a load moves, you increase the force for the same work done or energy used. So a screw with a lot of turns is easier to drive in than one of the same length with only a few.

A car jack uses the same principle. The threads are very close together so that the car can be lifted with a small force.

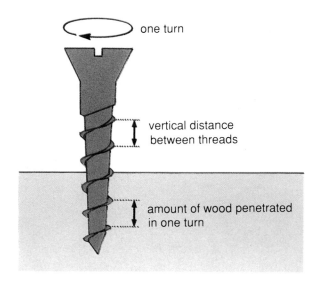

Above A diagram to show how a screw works. In one turn, the screw penetrates the wood by the same distance as that between each thread.

Below A selection of screws.

ACTIVITY

MAKING MODEL SCREWS

YOU NEED

- **a pencil**
- **paper**
- **a ruler**
- **scissors**
- **a red crayon**

1 Measure the length of your pencil.
2 Draw right-angled triangles on the paper, each with the same vertical height as the length of your pencil.
3 Make each triangle have a different slope.

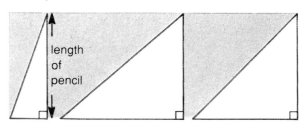

4 Measure the length of each slope. Notice that these slopes are ramps.

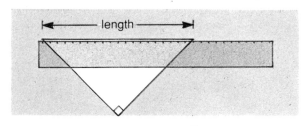

5 Use a red crayon to draw along each slope.

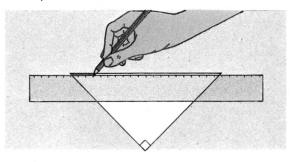

6 Carefully cut out each paper ramp.
7 Wind one triangle tightly around the pencil. Notice the rod spiral, which was the slope of your ramp. You have made a model screw.

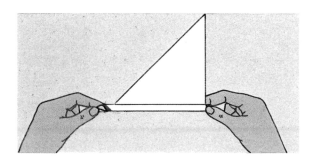

8 Measure the number of turns there are in the length of the pencil. Measure the number of turns there are per centimetre. This is the pitch of the thread. Do this for all your paper ramps. What do you notice?
9 Which model screw would be the easiest to screw in, and why?

TEST YOURSELF

1. Explain how a screw works.
2. What is the pitch of the thread of a screw?
3. Explain how it is possible for someone to lift a heavy car using a car jack.

ROLLERS AND WHEELS

You have probably noticed how hard it is to push a heavy load along the ground. You have to use a lot of effort to get it moving. This is because you are battling against two forces: the force of the load and another force, called friction. This is the force that occurs when two objects are rubbed together (in this case, the ground and the load where they touch each other). A lot of energy is used to overcome this friction and keep the load moving.

You can cut down friction by putting a heavy load on rollers, which turn as the load moves. Now the rollers are between the load and the ground. As a roller is a cylinder, only a small part of it is in contact with the ground at any time. Wheels are really narrow rollers, so the contact area is reduced even

more. This reduces friction to a very low level. Wheels can be fixed to a load with axles that join the wheels together. Another way of attaching the wheels is to make a cart, which is a box on wheels. You still have to use energy to move the cart and the load, so the lighter the wheels and the cart, the less energy you have to use to move them.

Wheels can be made lighter using spokes instead of solid wheels. Using modern, strong, light metals, very light wheels can be made. Examine the wheels on your bicycle to see how light they are. Almost all vehicles run on wheels. How many different kinds of wheel have you moved on this week?

This Canadian truck moves more easily on wheels, which reduce friction.

ACTIVITY

USING ROLLERS

YOU NEED

- **a rubber balloon**
- **a lightweight cardboard box**
- **a box of drinking straws**
- **20 cylindrical pencils or thin rods**
- **20 marbles of the same size**
- **scissors**
- **a ruler**

1 Use scissors to make a hole at one end of a cardboard box.

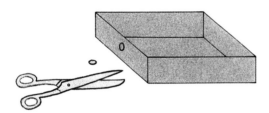

2 Put the balloon in the box. Poke the neck of the balloon through the hole in the box.

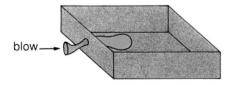

blow ⟶

3 Blow up the balloon in the box and twist the neck to keep in the air.

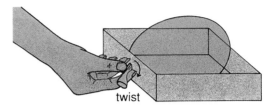

twist

4 Place a row of plastic drinking straws on a table.
5 Place the box on the straws. Untwist the neck of the balloon. Let it go.

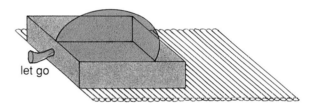

let go

6 In which direction does the box travel? In which direction does the air leave the balloon? What happens to the straws?
7 Repeat this experiment using the pencils instead of the straws. What happens?
8 Repeat this experiment using marbles instead of pencils. The marbles will need to be put carefully onto the table or they will roll off.
9 Repeat this experiment without the straws, pencils or marbles. Which method works best? Why?

TEST YOURSELF

1. Why is it difficult to push or pull a load up an inclined plane?
2. How do rollers or wheels help in moving a load up an inclined plane?

STORING ENERGY

Energy is used to blow up the balloon. It stores this energy until the air is released.

Rubber is an elastic material. This is something that can spring back to its original shape, after its shape has been changed by a force. Elastic materials can store energy. If you stretch rubber, you use force to stretch it to a certain distance. You do work to stretch the rubber, and, as on page 12:

work done = force x the distance that the rubber is stretched

The work done is the same as the energy used. Therefore, energy is needed to stretch rubber. This is kinetic (moving) energy. It can then be transferred to the rubber, where it is stored as potential energy. This can be released as kinetic energy again, as soon as the rubber springs back to its original shape.

If you blow up a balloon, you transfer energy to it. This energy is then stored in the balloon, until the neck is opened and the air escapes. As it does so, the balloon returns to its original shape, and flies about the room. This shows that the balloon has movement energy.

Rubber balloons and rubber bands are able to store energy and release it, so they are a very useful power source for models. Metal can be made into springs, which can be wound up. The winding is movement energy, which is stored in the tightly-coiled spring. When the spring is released, it unwinds, giving movement energy. This can be used to run small machines, such as watches and toy cars.

ACTIVITY

MAKING A STORED-ENERGY TOY

YOU NEED

- **a cotton reel**
- **a hacksaw**
- **a knife**
- **a candle**
- **a used matchstick**
- **a thin nail**
- **a strong rubber band**

1 Use the hacksaw to cut a groove across one end of the cotton reel. Check that the nail fits into this groove.

2 Use the knife to cut a thick slice from the candle.

3 Use the nail to make a hole in the middle of the candle slice.

4 Push the rubber band through the cotton reel.

5 Fasten one end of the rubber band to the nail. Let the nail fit into the groove in the cotton reel.

6 Pass the other end of the rubber band through the candle slice and fasten it to a matchstick at the other end.

7 Turn the matchstick to wind up the rubber band.

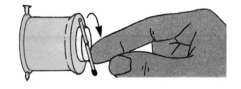

8 Put your toy on the floor. Release it. What happens?

9 Can your toy travel over rough surfaces and up steep slopes?

WARNING: be very careful when using the knife and the saw.

TEST YOURSELF

1. Explain how a rubber band can store energy.
2. Explain how a toy, using a rubber band as an energy source, works. Describe how the energy is changed from one form to another.

ENERGY TRANSFER

When we say that energy is used, we do not mean that it is used up or that there is less of it. Energy is never destroyed; it is only changed from one form to another. Energy is never created; again, it is only changed from one form of energy to another. For example, the energy from the Sun is transformed into chemical energy by green plants (see page 6). Animals eat plants, and we eat the animals and plants. This is called energy transfer and is how we obtain the energy to do things, such as ride a bicycle.

Think of all the energy transfers that happen when a light bulb is made to glow. It is a very complicated path, but, basically, it starts with the Sun's energy. The Sun's energy helps green plants to grow (chemical energy). When they die, some plants (over thousands of years) become coal. The coal is mined and may be burnt in a power station, changing the chemical energy into heat and light. This is used to turn water into steam. The steam rotates a turbine (kinetic energy). The turbine turns a generator to give electrical energy. This is passed to the light bulb, where it heats a wire, which glows brightly, giving light energy.

All the simple machines that we have used take in one form of energy and transfer it to a more useful form. Levers, inclined planes, screws, jacks, rollers and wheels only transfer energy; they do not produce or destroy it. Each time we use one of these machines to transfer energy, some of that energy is changed to heat or sound energy. The energy 'lost' as heat or sound is due to friction.

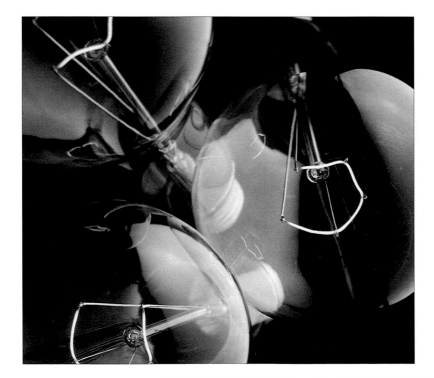

The electrical energy that reaches a light bulb is converted into light and heat energy in the tiny coil of wire inside the glass.

ACTIVITY

USING FRICTION FOR ENERGY TRANSFER

YOU NEED

- **4 cotton reels**
- **a candle**
- **a hammer**
- **a knife**
- **4 nails, longer than the cotton reels**
- **a thick block of wood**
- **rubber bands**

1 Cut 4 slices from a candle.
2 Put a nail through 1 cotton reel and through the middle of 1 candle slice.

 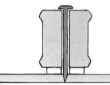

3 Hammer the nail into the wood. Check that the reel turns freely on the nail.
4 Repeat this for the second cotton reel. Hammer this nail into the wood so that the 2 cotton reels touch.

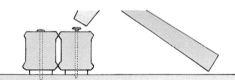

5 Turn the first cotton reel. What happens to the other one?
6 Wind a rubber band around the first reel, where the 2 reels touch.

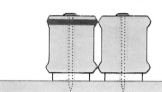

7 Turn the first reel. What happens to the second reel?
8 Hammer the nail of the third reel into the wood, so that all 3 reels touch.

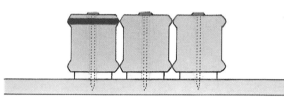

9 Turn the first reel. Which way do the other reels turn?
10 Turn the second reel. Which way do the other reels turn?
11 Can you predict which way the other reels turn if you move the third one?

WARNING: be very careful when using the hammer and the knife.

TEST YOURSELF

1. Is it possible to get more energy out of a machine than you put into it? Explain your answer.
2. Give an example of how one form of energy is transformed into two other forms of energy.
3. Explain how friction can be used to transfer energy.

PULLEYS

Wheels can not only be used to move a load along the ground; they can also be used to raise a load up in the air. A pulley is a wheel with a groove around the rim for carrying a belt, rope or chain. A single, fixed pulley is often used to lift loads up tall buildings. A rope is passed around the pulley and a load is attached to one end. The load is raised by pulling on the other end of the rope.

The pulley is just like the fulcrum on a first-class lever (see page 14). The effort is made on one side of the pulley and the load moves in the opposite direction on the other side. The effort force has to be greater than the load force, if the load is to be moved. This does not seem a very efficient machine, as the effort force has not only to raise the load, but also to overcome the friction force in the pulley and the friction between the rope and the pulley. However, the advantage is that it is easier for the worker to pull down on the rope, using the strength of the body with the help of gravity, than it is to carry the load up the ladder.

A more efficient system is found in a moveable pulley. Here, the pulley system works like a second-class lever (see page 14). Here, the effort is made in the same direction as the load is moving. The rope is fixed at one end and the pulley with the load runs along the rope. When the other end of the rope is lifted, the pulley and the load are lifted. A great deal more movement has to be made on the effort side than on the load side.
Remember that:

Work done = effort (force) x distance

Therefore, if the effort end of the rope is pulled up through a large distance, the effort force is not so large as with a fixed pulley.

This worker on the Mackinac Bridge in Michigan, USA, is using a pulley system to lift himself up to a girder.

ACTIVITY

A MOVEABLE PULLEY

YOU NEED

- **a cotton reel**
- **20 cm of stiff wire**
- **a long length of string**
- **a load, such as a heavy book**
- **pliers**
- **a ruler**
- **a newtonmeter**

1 Pass the wire through the reel.
2 Use pliers to join the ends of the wire together to form a hook.

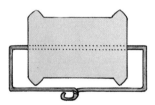

3 Tie string around the book or weight. Attach the string to the newtonmeter. Raise the book and measure the force needed on the newtonmeter.

4 Remove the newtonmeter and attach the book to the pulley hook.
5 Tie another length of string to a door handle. Pass the string through the pulley and attach it to the newtonmeter.

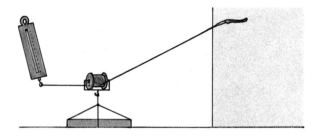

6 Pull on the string to raise the book. Measure how much force is needed this time.
7 Is the book easier to lift with or without the pulley?
8 Ask a friend to measure how far the string was pulled to lift the book 10 cm.

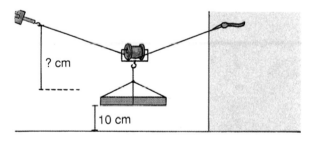

Repeat these measurements for vertical lifts of 20 cm, 30 cm, 40 cm, and 50 cm. What do you notice about the distance that the string was pulled in relation to the height that the book was raised?

TEST YOURSELF

1. What is a pulley?
2. Describe how you would use a single, fixed pulley.
3. Why does a moveable pulley need less effort than a fixed pulley?

MULTIPLE PULLEY SYSTEMS

In a single, fixed pulley, the effort and load forces are almost the same, and the distances that the effort and the load move are the same (see page 32). However, if two pulleys are used – one fixed and one moveable – the system can be made more efficient. The fixed pulley causes the load to be lifted. The moveable pulley is also raised with the load, as the effort is pulled down. Here, you will find that the effort force needs to move down twice as far as the moveable pulley and load go up.

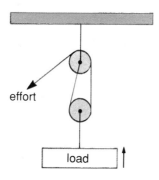

To show how this machine is more efficient, suppose that a mass of 6 kg is put on the effort side. This is a force of 60 newtons (see page 18). It will balance and lift a load of 12 kg (a load force of 120 newtons). This means that half the effort is needed to lift the load.

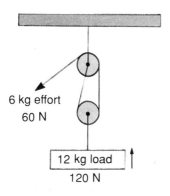

If a second moveable pulley is added, a mass of 4 kg (an effort force of 40 newtons) will balance the load of 12 kg. Here, the effort moves three times as far as the load.

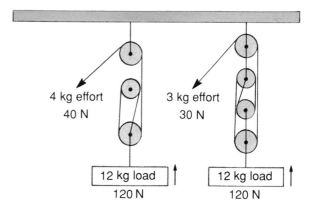

If a third moveable pulley is added to the system, then 3 kg (an effort force of 30 newtons) is needed to balance the 12 kg load. Here, the effort moves four times the distance of the load. Notice that:

load force ÷ effort force = number of pulleys

This way, you can work out how many pulleys you need to lift a particular load. However, this is for a system that has no friction. All pulley systems have friction, so you have to allow for this, by adding another pulley or increasing the effort force. In a block-and-tackle system, the pulleys may be difficult to count, so count the number of times that the rope turns around a pulley. These systems are used on sailing ships. One sailor can use this sort of pulley system to move many sails.

ACTIVITY

YOU NEED

- **two long, smooth broom handles**
- **a length of strong rope**
- **some friends**

1 Tie a length of rope tightly to one end of a broom handle.
2 Ask your friends to hold the handles horizontal and about 1 m apart. The broom handles will act as pulleys.
3 Wind the rope around the handles 6 times.

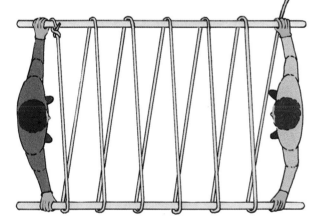

4 Tell your friends not to move while you pull on the rope. What happens?

5 Wind the rope around the handles a few more times.
6 Ask more friends to hold the handles.
7 Pull on the rope. Can you move 4 friends?
8 To calculate whether you can move your friends, count the number of times that the rope is wound around the handles. The number of turns of the rope is the same as the number of pulleys. Remember: you have to allow for the friction force between the turns of the rope and the broom handles, but 8 or 10 turns should move 4 friends easily. Try it.

WARNING: take great care when doing this activity. Make sure that an adult is there to help you.

TEST YOURSELF

1. When and where are multiple pulley systems used?
2. If a system contained 4 pulleys, how much effort would be needed to balance a load of 400 newtons, assuming that there was no friction?
3. If the effort moved 8 m, how far would the load move?

PULLEYS OF DIFFERENT SIZES

Pulleys need not be the same size. Suppose that we have two pulleys: one has a diameter of 20 cm and the other has a diameter of 5 cm. Therefore, one is four times larger than the other. Join the two pulleys together, so that they rotate together. Now put them on a spindle, or axle, to make two fixed

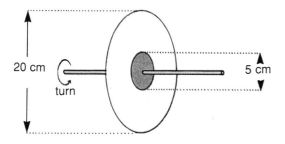

pulleys. If the large pulley turns around once, the small pulley will have turned around four times. Also, the small pulley will move four times as fast as the large pulley. Try this with pulleys made of cardboard.

You can find pulley systems rather like this in a car engine. Two pulleys are joined by the fan belt. The large pulley is attached to the motor. As the engine turns, so does the large pulley. This drives the small pulley attached to the fan. The fan then rotates very quickly to cool the engine.

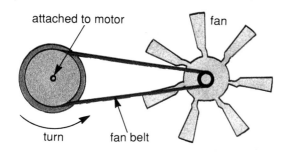

Look at the pedals on your bicycle. They can be thought of as being a large pulley. They are attached to the drive wheel, which is the toothed metal wheel that carries the chain. If the drive wheel and the pedals are connected, then one turn of the pedals gives one turn of the drive wheel. Because the

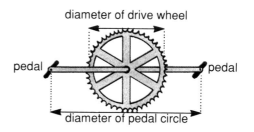

pedal circle is larger than the drive wheel, the force generated by your legs is effectively increased. The drive wheel is connected to a smaller pulley – the cog in the back wheel. They turn at the same time, because of the chain that connects them.

Here, again, a large pulley turns a small pulley, so the bicycle moves very quickly for your effort force. A pedal is not really a pulley, although it works in the same way. A pedal and drive wheel acting together are known as a crank.

ACTIVITY

USING A CRANK

YOU NEED

- **a large cork**
- **20 cm of strong, thick steel wire**
- **a large paper clip**
- **thread**
- **a heavy book**
- **pliers**
- **sticky tape**

1 Push the wire carefully through the middle of the cork, so that the cork acts as an axle.
2 Put one end of a length of thread on the cork. Tape it to the cork to prevent it from slipping.
3 Wind the thread twice around the cork and let it hang down.

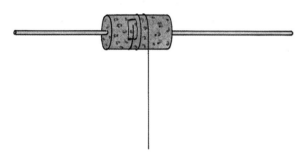

4 Make a hook from the paper clip.
5 Tie the hook to the end of the thread.

6 Tie another length of thread around the hook.
7 Hang the book from the hook.

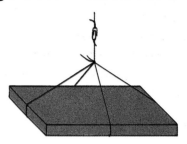

8 Bend one end of the wire with the pliers to make a crank.

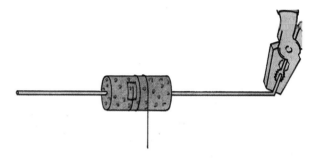

9 Ask a friend to hold the wire straight.
10 Turn the crank to raise the book.
11 Bend the wire to make a larger crank. It is easier or harder to lift the book?

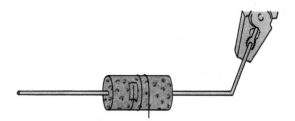

TEST YOURSELF

1. How are pulleys used in a car engine to drive the fan?
2. A 12 cm-diameter pulley is fixed to a 6 cm-diameter pulley. If the larger pulley turns once in 1 second, how fast does the small pulley turn?
3. Explain how using a crank handle can help you to lift a load.

GEARS

Lubricating oil can be put on gear teeth to help reduce friction. The force of friction always converts movement energy to heat energy.

You have found out that, by using pulleys of different sizes, large loads can be lifted without needing a large number of pulleys. Pulleys of different sizes can also be made to rotate at different speeds. However, pulleys are connected with ropes or belts. If a large load is put on a pulley, or it rotates very quickly, the rope or belt may slip. To prevent slipping, a lot of friction force is needed. This converts a great deal of the effort force into heat, so the energy being used to do the work is being turned into heat energy. This is 'wasted' energy; you are turning some of your energy into something you do not want.

Gears were invented to improve this. They are pulleys that have teeth all around the rim. These teeth mesh with the teeth of other gears so that they cannot slip. You can put lubricating oil on the teeth to make them mesh smoothly and cut down friction. With friction reduced, very little effort is turned to heat. A lot less energy is 'wasted': that is, changed into an

energy that you do not want.

The rate at which gear wheels turn depends on the number of teeth on each gear. Compare two gears: one with 20 teeth and one with 40. If the gear with 40 teeth turns once, the gear with 20 teeth turns twice. Also, the smaller gear turns twice as fast as the larger gear.

Gears are found in many machines, such as bicycles and cars. They are used so that a small effort is needed to drive a large load, or to move it quickly.

ACTIVITY

MAKING GEAR WHEELS

YOU NEED

- **corrugated cardboard**
- **scissors**
- **sticky tape**
- **a screwdriver**
- **a hammer**
- **nails**
- **wood**
- **2 cans of different diameters**
- **screws**

1 Wrap the corrugated cardboard once around each can, with the corrugations on the outside.

2 Tape the ends of the cardboard together and tape the cardboard to the cans.

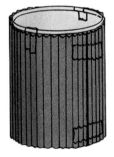

3 Check that the cardboard teeth on the cans mesh.

4 Hammer a nail into the middle of the base of each can, to make a large hole for a screw.

5 Screw one can on to the wood. Screw the next can to it, so that the corrugated cardboard teeth mesh.

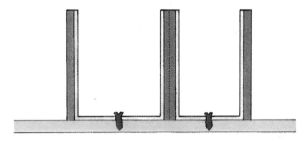

6 Turn the larger can. Does the other can turn faster or slower?

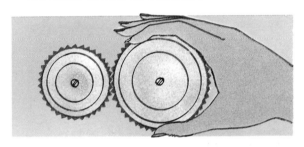

7 Mark one gear tooth on each can. Count the number of gear teeth on each can.

8 See how many times the smaller can moves if the other is moved around once.

WARNING: be very careful when using a hammer.

TEST YOURSELF

1. What advantage have gear wheels over pulley wheels?

2. If a large gear wheel of 30 teeth is meshed with a small gear wheel of 10 teeth, how many times does the other gear wheel turn when
- the small gear wheel turns once?
- the large gear wheel turns once?

ENERGY IS CONSERVED

You have already discovered that energy is conserved (see page 30). This means that it is not created or destroyed; it is just changed from one form to another. There are many types of energy change. You have seen how machines use energy. For example, if you are riding a bicycle, you must move your legs (movement, or kinetic energy) to transfer the energy to drive the wheel. This, in turn, transfers the movement energy to the back wheel cog, which transfers it to the wheels. The movement energy is then used, mostly, to move the bicycle along.

An efficient machine is one that transfers the energy to do the task that we want. Ideally only a little of the energy is wasted as heat energy due to friction. A bicycle is, therefore, an efficient machine; only about 5 per cent of the input energy (the energy from your muscles) is converted to heat energy by the drive mechanism.

This 'energy loss' is due to friction in the drive-wheel bearings, the chain, the gear wheel and the rear-wheel bearings. Some of the friction is useful in keeping your feet on the pedals and the wheels on the road.

An energy transfer where we want to produce heat can be very efficient. An electric immersion heater converts electricity almost totally to heat energy. It is only when we store the hot water that heat energy is 'lost' through the tank insulation and into the air.

A car is a very inefficient machine. In burning the fuel, a great deal of energy is lost as heat. The engine needs to be cooled, so more energy is lost in the cooling system.

There are many other ways in which energy is transferred. See how many you can think of. Different forms of energy include light, heat, sound, chemical, electrical, and mechanical (kinetic and potential).

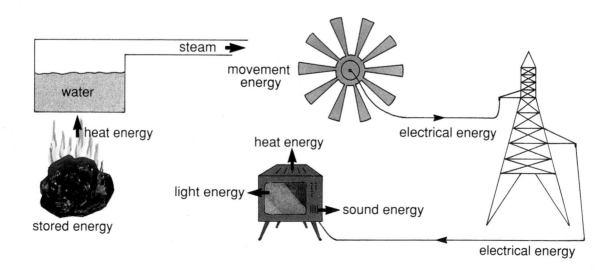

ACTIVITY

MEASURING HEAT ENERGY

> ### YOU NEED
>
> - **3 washing-up bowls**
> - **hot and cold water**
> - **a thermometer**

1 Put water into each bowl, so that each is half full. Put cold water into one, tepid water into another and very warm water into the third. Do not make the third bowl too hot.

2 Put your left hand in the cold water and your right hand into the very warm water. What do you feel?

3 Keep your hands under the water for 5 minutes.
4 Now bring your hands out of the water and put them both into the tepid water.

5 What do you feel in your right hand? What do you feel in your left hand?
6 Put the thermometer into the cold water. What temperature is it? Take the temperature of the tepid water and the very warm water. Record these temperatures.
7 Take the temperature of the 3 bowls of water every 5 minutes. What happens? Why?

Temperature (°C)	Start	5 mins	10 mins
cold			
tepid			
very warm			

8 Take the temperature of the 3 bowls after a few hours. Compare these temperatures with that of the air in the room. What do you notice? Notice that whether the water seems hot or cold depends first on the relationship to our bodies. It feels hot or cold in relation to us. It also depends upon which temperature we felt last. So the tepid water feels cool to one hand and warm to the other.

> WARNING: be very careful when using hot water.

TEST YOURSELF

1. Explain what is meant by an efficient machine.
2. Describe the energy transfer path from you to your moving bicycle. Where does your energy come from? See page 30 to help with your answer.
3. There is never a beginning or an end to an energy transfer path. Why?

HEAT ENERGY TRAVELS

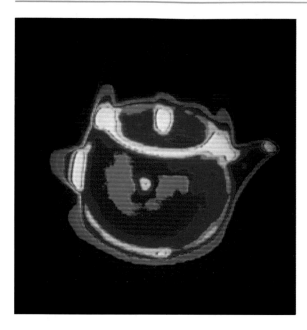

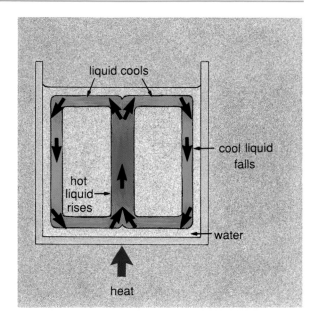

Above *A diagram to show convection.*

Left *This special photograph shows how heat is conducted in a kettle that has just been switched on. The hottest areas appear white, while the coldest are blue.*

You know that heat is a form of energy. Like light, it travels as a mass of waves. Heat travels at the speed of light, which is very fast. As it travels, it spreads out in all directions. Heat always moves, or transfers energy, from a warm place to somewhere cooler. When we say that something will 'let in the cold', we are wrong; it is the heat that is being let out.

When heat from the Sun reaches us across space, it is travelling from the hot Sun to somewhere cooler, (in this case, the Earth). The heat from the Sun spreads out in all directions, not just towards us. Energy travelling like this is called radiation. Light and sound behave in exactly the same way.

If heat energy meets a solid, it will pass into the solid and through it, moving from the hottest point to the coolest. Heat travelling this way in a solid is called conduction.

Heat energy waves passing into gases or liquids cause convection currents. As the hot gas or liquid heats up, it becomes less dense and rises. It is replaced by the surrounding cooler gas or liquid. If you heat water in a pan on a stove, the water at the bottom of the pan gets hot first and rises up. The cold water at the top sinks down, to be heated by the stove. In this way, the water circles round until the panful is hot enough. Similarly, when the Sun heats the land, the air above the land rises to form a convection current. Gliders and birds are able to circle in these rising air convection currents.

No matter how heat travels, whether by radiation, conduction or convection, it always moves from hot to cold.

ACTIVITY

CONDUCTION

YOU NEED

- **a long metal knitting needle**
- **a large metal tray**
- **sand**
- **pins**
- **petroleum jelly**
- **a large pair of pliers**
- **a candle**
- **a candle holder**
- **matches**

1 Put sand in the large metal tray.
2 Put the candle in the candle holder and stand it on the tray.

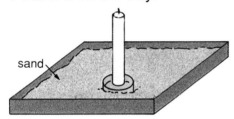

3 Measure the long knitting needle and mark it at 3 cm intervals.

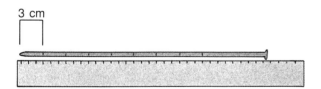

4 Ask a friend to hold one end of the needle while you stick on a pin, at each 3 cm mark, with petroleum jelly.

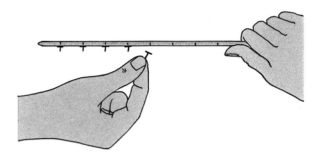

5 Ask your friend to light the candle.
6 Hold the needle at one end, using the pliers.
7 Put the other end of the needle in the candle flame. Hold the needle still. What happens?

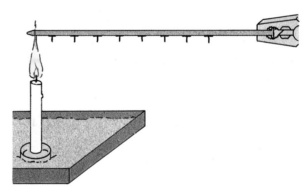

WARNING: you must not attempt this activity without the help of an adult.

TEST YOURSELF

1. What is heat?
2. Name three ways in which heat can travel.
3. Why are the handles of metal saucepans usually made of wood or plastic?

CHANGING STATE

Everything is made of tiny particles called atoms, which join to make molecules. These molecules constantly vibrate with kinetic (movement) energy. In a solid, the molecules form a pattern, which gives the solid its shape. They are rather like bricks packed together

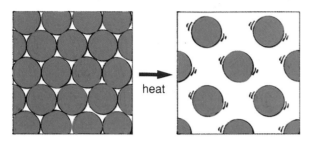

in a pattern to form a building. When heat waves hit the molecules, the energy in the heat waves changes to kinetic energy, making the molecules move faster and further. This means that they are more likely to bump into each other, so they take up more space to allow for this. This increase is called expansion, and the whole solid becomes larger. It is like a roomful of people who are moving about quickly; they need more space, or they will bump into each other.

Liquids and gases also expand when they get hotter. They become less dense and rise up, forming convection currents (see page 42). Hot air expands; that is why hot-air balloons rise.

Heat energy can also change the state (solid, liquid or gas) of a substance. For example, ice is solid water. When the molecules of ice are heated, they move faster. They take up more space. There are connections between the molecules, which are called bonds. As the molecules move faster and further, the bonds are weakened and the ice becomes liquid water. If the water is heated more, it

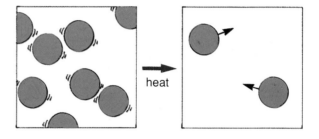

becomes hotter. The molecules in the water eventually have enough speed to break their bonds completely. They jump right out of the water to become the gas called steam. When the steam cools down, the molecules will move more and more slowly, and the steam condenses to water. When the water cools the molecules move more slowly still, until they freeze to form ice. As this cooling takes place, the kinetic energy of the molecules is transformed into heat energy again. This escapes into the surrounding air.

Hot air expands, becomes less dense and rises. This is why hot-air balloons fly.

ACTIVITY

YOU NEED

- **a heatproof glass pan or dish**
- **a heat source**
- **ice**
- **dark-coloured bath crystals**

1 Half fill the pan with ice. Put the pan with the ice on a very low heat.

2 Watch what happens by looking through the sides of the pan. Do not put your face near or over the pan.

3 Watch as the ice slowly melts. The ice will float in the water.

4 Once all the ice has melted, add a few bath crystals to the water.

5 Watch as the convection currents form in the water. You will see the dye from the crystals moving with the currents.

6 Watch the air bubbles form and rise to the surface. Gradually, as you continue to heat the water, it will begin to boil. Do not let it boil fiercely.

7 Watch as the water turns to steam. How do you know that it is the water that is making the steam?

8 Once some of the water has turned to steam, switch off your heat source and let the water cool down.

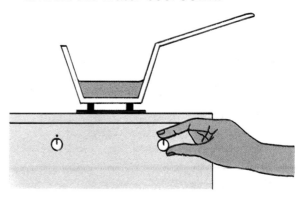

9 Will the water go back to the ice that you started with? Why? Can you get the steam back? Why? Where has all the heat from your heat source gone?

WARNING: you must not attempt this activity without the help of an adult.

TEST YOURSELF

1. What does heat do to molecules?
2. Describe how heat can change the state of materials.
3. Why do hot-air balloons rise?

Glossary

Accelerate To speed up.

Atom The smallest particle of an element that can take part in a chemical reaction.

Axle The pin or rod through a wheel. The wheel turns around the axle.

Bearings The part of a machine that is designed to reduce friction.

Condense To turn a gas into a liquid, either by pressure or by cooling.

Conduction (of heat) The transfer of heat in solids.

Conservation (of energy) Energy cannot be created or destroyed, only its form can be changed (e.g. movement energy to sound energy).

Convection The transfer of heat in a liquid or gas by the movement of the gas or liquid itself.

Crank A simple machine that increases the turning force.

Effort The force that is doing work on an object.

Energy A measure of the ability to do work, measured in joules.

Engine A machine for changing chemical energy (fuel) into movement energy.

Force A push, pull or resistance. It is measured in newtons.

Friction A force that occurs when two surfaces move across each other. It slows down movement. Heat energy is generated when this happens, and often sound energy.

Fuel An energy store that can be burnt to release the energy.

Fulcrum A pivot. A place at which a lever turns.

Gears Interlocking toothed wheels used for the transfer of energy.

Gravity The pulling force of the Earth and other solid bodies, such as the Sun.

Immersion heater An electrical heater placed in water to heat it up.

Inclined plane A wedge used to raise a load easily. The load moves, not the wedge.

Insulation (heat) The prevention of the passage of heat from, for example, a hot-water tank to its surroundings. It is also the material that is used for this purpose.

Jack A machine containing a screw thread, used for lifting loads.

Joule A unit of energy. One joule equals the work done when a force of one newton moves a 1-kg object by one metre.

Kinetic energy The energy of movement, measured in joules.

Lever A simple machine that changes the force applied.

Mass The amount of substance that a body contains, measured in kilograms.

Newton A unit of force. One newton is the force which acts on a mass of 1 kilogram to produce an acceleration (a speed increase) of 1 metre per second every second.

Pivot The point around which a wheel or lever turns.

Plane A flat or level surface.

Potential energy Mechanical energy that is stored due to either an object's position (e.g. a rock at the top of a cliff) or what has happened to an object (e.g. a stretched elastic band).

Pulley A grooved wheel carrying a rope, belt or chain.

Speed The average rate at which an object is travelling, measured in metres per second, kph, etc.

Turbine A machine for generating rotary movement. The blades of a turbine can be turned by air, gas, steam or a liquid.

Wedge A simple machine, consisting of a triangular block that is pushed into a gap, increasing the force.

Weight The force exerted by gravity on an object. It is measured in newtons.

Work This is done when a force is moved over a certain distance. Energy is used when work is done, and it is measured in joules.

Books to read

Balls and Balloons Ed Catherall (Wayland, 1985)

Energy from the Sun Jan Burgess (Macmillan, 1987)

Friction Ed Catherall (Wayland, 1983)

How Machines Work Christopher Rawson (Usborne, 1988)

How Things Work Martyn Bramwell (Usborne, 1984)

Mechanics Steve Parker (Granada, 1985)

The Science of Movement Ralph Hancock (Macmillan, 1984)

Simple Mechanics John Paull and Dorothy Paull (Ladybird, 1982)

Picture acknowledgements

The author and publishers would like to thank the following for allowing illustrations to be reproduced in this book: Eye Ubiquitous *cover*, 24, 28; Trevor Hill 20; PHOTRI 16, 30; Science Photo Library 42; Topham 10; Wayland Picture Library *frontispiece*, 6, 17 (Michael Dent), 26 (Chris Fairclough); ZEFA *cover*, 7, 8, 9, 12, 14, 22, 28, 32, 44. All artwork is by Jenny Hughes.

Index